101 ways
TO CELEBRATE
God's Special Day!

ℝ

REVIEW AND HERALD® PUBLISHING ASSOCIATION

Since 1861 | www.reviewandherald.com

Check out these other great books from *Guide* magazine!

Guide's Greatest Series:
   Prayer Stories
   Miracle Stories
   Escape From Crime Stories
   Sabbath Stories
   Christmas Stories
   Angel Stories
   Animal Stories
   Mystery Stories
   Narrow Escape Stories
   Grace Stories

Guide's True Story Series:
   Just Plane Crazy
   Finding My Way in Milwaukee
   Katya's Gold

Other Books:
   Elasti-Brain: 365 Devotions
     to Stretch Your Mind
     and Shape Your Faith

Copyright © 2008 by Review and Herald® Publishing Association

Published by Review and Herald® Publishing Association, Hagerstown, MD 21741-1119

Review and Herald® titles may be purchased in bulk for educational, business, fund-raising, or sales promotional use. For information, please e-mail SpecialMarkets@reviewandherald.com.

The Review and Herald® Publishing Association publishes biblically based materials for spiritual, physical, and mental growth and Christian discipleship.

The author assumes full responsibility for the accuracy of all facts and quotations as cited in this book.

Texts credited to NIV are from the *Holy Bible, New International Version.* Copyright © 1973, 1978, 1984, International Bible Society. Used by permission of Zondervan Bible Publishers.

This book was
Edited by JoAlyce Waugh
Copyedited by James Cavil
Designed by Ron J. Pride
Cover photos © iStockphoto
*Special thanks to Mrs. Benton's 5th, 6th, and 7th grade classes at Mount Aetna Elementary School
   for their Sabbath Action suggestions.*
Interior designed by Heather Rogers
Typeset: Helvetica Condensed 12/15

PRINTED IN U.S.A.

12 11 10 09 08   5 4 3 2 1

Library of Congress Cataloging-in-Publication Data
Guide magazine presents— Sabbath action blast! : 101 ways to celebrate God's special day.
   p. cm.
1. Church work with youth—Seventh-day Adventists. 2. Church work with children—Seventh-day Adventists. 3. Sabbath. I. Review and Herald Publishing Association. II. Guide magazine. III. Title: Sabbath action blast!
   BV4447.G85 2008
   263'.1—dc22

                    2008029005

ISBN 978-0-8280-2368-9

CONTENTS

* Requires materials you may need to gather in advance.
+ Requires advance planning and/or preparation.

GUIDE

DECLARES WAR ON SABBATH BOREDOM!

That's how we announced our campaign to help *Guide* readers turn their Sabbaths into something more than a day filled with things they couldn't do.

The book you now hold in your hands is the end result of that effort. All the activities originally appeared in the magazine, and were submitted by a wide range of young people and adults.

There are nearly two years' worth of fun Sabbath activities in this collection. We trust they'll help you in your efforts to energize the Sabbath for young people.

—The *Guide* Editors

For more great Sabbath Action Blast activities, go to
www.guidemagazine.org

THE THREE-HEADED STORYTELLER
—Heather Down

Choose a "show host" and three participants. The host decides on a Bible story that the three participants must tell in their own words. The only catch is they can say only one word at a time. Going in order, they must completely relate the Bible story given to them by the host.

Option: Make it more challenging by having them sing the story instead. Try it with your family for sundown worship!

Picture This!
—Ron Reese

Choose a Bible text (or other cool quote) you'd like to learn, and draw pictures to stand for letters or sounds in words. For example, for the first few words of John 3:16 (KJV) you could draw: 4 God (picture of needle and thread) (picture of heart + ed) the (picture of globe) (t + picture of hat) he (picture of arms reaching out with a gift).

Try it with a friend and see if you can each figure out the other's verse.

SABBATH ACTION BLAST 3

PHOTO VISION

—Ernst Louis-Jacques

You will need:

- *two digital cameras*
- *notepad or chalkboard*
- *timer*

*F*or this game you will need two teams, each with about two to three players. (It helps if one player is an adult.)

This game begins with each team going outside and taking five pictures. These pictures should show how you see God in nature. It makes the game more fun if the pictures are weird-looking (close-up, unique perspective, etc.).

When the teams are finished taking pictures, everyone should gather in one place. One team shows their pictures while the other team guesses what the objects are. They have two minutes and three guesses per picture. If the team runs out of guesses, the team that took the picture tells what the object is and explains what that object tells them about God.

Each correct guess is worth two points. On the notepad or chalkboard, tally the points for each team. The team with the most points wins.

SCRIPTURE SCAVENGER HUNT

—Violet Nesdoly

You will need at least two individuals or teams for this hunt. Each person or team will need:

- *a New International Version Bible*
- *a paper or plastic bag to hold their collection*

1. Look up the Bible verse clues.
2. Pick out the object named in each verse. (If several objects are named, choose one to find.)
3. Find the objects and place them in the bag. The person or team done first wins!

Scripture clues:

Psalm 139:18	Luke 15:9	1 Samuel 17:18
Matthew 5:13	Psalm 119:103	Job 13:25
Psalm 144:1	Acts 13:25	Exodus 32:32
James 1:10	Proverbs 1:14	Mark 14:4
Mark 6:39	Psalm 91:4	

Quick Draw

—Heather Down

ho is the quickest on the draw? Try this game to find out who s the fastest fingers.

1. Pick a person to be the mediator. That person makes a list of 10 different Bible objects or events: for example, the burning bush, the parting of the Red Sea, the stable in which Jesus was born.
2. Divide the rest of your group into two teams on separate sides of the room. Each team will need a writing instrument and some paper.
3. The mediator sits in the center with the list, hiding all but the first item.
4. When the mediator says "Go," one member from each team comes to find out the first item. They must then draw a picture of it for their team. When their team guesses it, a second team member goes and gets the next item to draw, and so on. Each team member must take a turn drawing.
5. The first team that completes and guesses the list is the winner.

WALDENSIANS IN THE WILDERNESS

—Janelle Wahlman

SABBATH ACTION BLAST 6

You will need:

- *copies of 10 different Scripture promises—enough for each Waldensian*
- *map of safe zones—enough for each Waldensian*
- *10 containers*

This game takes its name from a group of Reformation-era Christians who spread God's Word despite persecution. Bibles were scarce, so the Waldensians memorized large portions of Scripture.

The game is best played in a large outdoor area with lots of hiding places. Players are divided into two teams, soldiers and Waldensians. Prior to the game, the leader—who will not be on either team—marks 10 safe zones spaced throughout the play area. The soldiers are not allowed to know ahead of time where these safe zones are. At each safe zone, place copies of a different short Scripture promise inside a container. Include enough copies for each of the Waldensians.

At the starting point (the first safe zone) the Waldensians are given the first Scripture promise and a map of the safe zones. The object is for the Waldensians to collect all 10 Scripture promises, memorize as many as possible, and make it safely to a designated finish zone.

The Waldensians are allowed a five-minute head start, and the soldiers may not watch where they go. The Waldensians may remain up to five minutes at a time at each safe zone to work on memorizing each Scripture promise. Five minutes after the start of the game, the soldiers may begin to hunt and capture Waldensians by tagging

WALDENSIANS IN THE WILDERNESS CONTINUED

them between safe zones. (A soldier is not allowed to remain at the safe zone waiting for the Waldensians!)

When Waldensians are tagged, they may go free by quoting one of the Scripture promises collected. Players may repeat each verse only once unless they have been caught so many times that they've quoted all the verses. If a tagged player cannot quote a Scripture promise, the player must give up one Scripture slip, return to the starting zone, and wait five minutes before starting again. The leader returns the slip to the correct safe zone.

To finish, Waldensians must collect the Scripture slip from each safe zone and cross the finish line with all slips in hand or memorized. Waldensians who finish may return to the playing field as the partner of another player. When their partner is tagged, the person who finished previously may help by quoting a Scripture promise. (A player who has finished may not be sent back to the starting zone.)

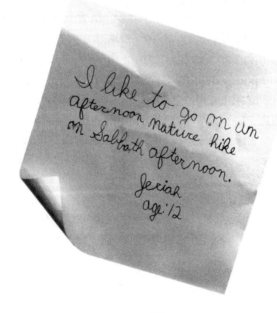

GUESS THIS TUNE

—Heather Down

Play a game of Guess This Tune with family or friends. You will need either a piano or CDs of familiar or not-so-familiar Christian music. Divide your group into two teams. Play a note or two of a song on the piano or a second or two on the CD. Have each team guess. If neither side gets it right, add a note or play the CD a little more.

When a side actually guesses it, you can continue by singing along with the song!

POTLUCK VISITORS

—Heather Down

You'll need an emcee and four actors for this make-it-up-as-you-go skit. One actor is the host of a potluck. The other three actors are given a secret name of a Bible character or other spiritual role model chosen by the emcee.

One by one the three actors ring the doorbell and enter the potluck. They must act and talk like their character without saying their names aloud. For instance, if you were Peter, you might talk about fishing or about miracles you'd seen Jesus perform.

The hosts (and other guests) then guess who they are.

GREAT LEAPS

—Adapted from *Non-Competitive Games*, Susan Butler, compiler (Bethany House Publishers, 1986).

In 1 Corinthians 12:27 Paul wrote, "Now you are the body of Christ, and each one of you is a part of it" (NIV).

When each part of the "body" does his or her job, amazing things will happen for Jesus! This activity is a good example of having fun while working together toward a common goal.

In an open area, create a starting line, and then have the first participant jump as far as possible from the line. Measure the length of the jump and mark the spot. Another person now jumps, and their measurement is added to the first one. All participants jump, and their total jump length is recorded.

Now go back and repeat the activity, trying to break the previous record. Do this as many times as you wish, or until you get sore!

Option: take turns flinging a Frisbee and see what total distance the group can achieve.

I like going horsebackriding everywhere!

Anbrielle
age: 12

Body Spell-It

—Adapted from Dan McGill, *No Supplies Required* (Group Publishing, 1995).

Can you write with your elbow? Sure, and here's a great way to prove it!

First, create about 20 cards or slips of paper on which different Sabbath-appropriate categories have been written, such as Animals, Foods in the Bible, Contemporary Christian Musicians, etc.

Now make another set of cards or slips of paper that each have one of the following body parts written on them: HEAD, RIGHT ELBOW, LEFT ELBOW, RIGHT LEG, LEFT LEG, RIGHT INDEX FINGER, LEFT INDEX FINGER, RIGHT KNEE, LEFT KNEE.

Place the category cards in one container and the body-parts cards in another. The first player draws out a category card and a body-parts card. The person silently decides on a word that fits the category chosen. He or she says the category out loud and then proceeds to "write" the word in midair for other players to guess, using only the body part designated on the card! The speller may not speak or make any sounds.

Optional: divide into teams and play like Pictionary, but with no paper or pencils!

CREATING ADAM

—Ron Reese

According to Ellen White's inspired writing, Adam "was more than twice as tall as men now living upon the earth" (*Spiritual Gifts*, vol. 3, p. 34). The average man today is about five feet 10 inches. So Adam was probably at least 12 feet tall!

Outside on the ground (the beach is a perfect place), measure how tall Adam would have been. Then use soil or sand to make a life-size sculpture of Adam. If you don't have access to soil or sand, use small stones, tape, or string to form the outline. When you're done, lie down beside your Adam, mark your height compared to his, and see what a shorty you are.

Read Genesis 2:7 about how God created Adam. Find the final key step that God performed—one you can't do!

BiG-SCREEN OUTREACH

—Ron Reese

Here's a great way to share your faith with your friends or kids in your neighborhood. Start a regular Sabbath afternoon "movie showing" in your home or at church. Invite people to come and watch a Christian video on a big-screen TV—or use a video projector if your church has one. You could even make up free "tickets" and pass them out to kids. Bring popcorn and drinks for everyone to enjoy while watching.

Illustrious Illusions

—Jason Down

13

This family worship activity requires some homework. Each family member has to find and practice a sleight-of-hand illusion that can be a spiritual object lesson. (Such "magic tricks" aren't actually magic, just illusions.) Public libraries and Internet sites* have some great ideas.

On the day of the worship each family member performs the trick, gives the object lesson, and shares a Bible verse that illustrates the point. Although some things may disappear during this activity, the lessons you learn won't!

*Try www.conjuror.com/magictricks/freetricks.shtml. To purchase Christian tricks, check out www.gospelmagic.com.

Lip-Sync Concert

—Violet Nesdoly

14

Mime your favorite Christian musician!

1. Listen to and learn the lyrics of a song done by your favorite Christian artist. Practice until you can move your lips perfectly along with the music.

2. Assemble concert props and costumes. You can fake-play real instruments, or use a cardboard or broom guitar, bucket drums, a jump-rope microphone—and of course, wigs and dress-up clothes for the singers.

3. Serenade your family and friends in a lip-sync concert.

4. *Optional: If you have access to a video camera, have a friend or family member videotape your performance and make your own music video.*

SHAMPOO GIVEAWAY

—Brenda Segna

1. Save the little soaps and shampoos from hotels when you're on family vacations, or purchase sample-size soaps, shampoos, deodorants, mouthwash, fragrance, etc., from a store. (Make your purchases sometime other than Sabbath! See Nehemiah 13:15-18.)
2. Decorate a paper bag with your favorite Bible verse, a positive quote/saying, or a picture drawn by you.
3. Deliver the bags to a women's/homeless shelter. The people who stay there will appreciate a touch of "luxury."
4. Most shelters are in need of help to serve meals. If you deliver the bags during mealtime, volunteer to serve.
5. Save all of your old *Guides* and donate them to the shelters as well! Doing a simple of act of kindness shares a glimpse of Jesus.

POOR MAN'S DVD PLAYER

—Randy Fishell

This device is called a zoetrope, and it really does animate your drawings!

You will need:
- *tape*
- *craft knife*
- *thick paper or thin cardboard*
- *lazy Susan or other turning platform*

Poor Man's DVD Player CONTINUED

Step 1: Cut enough strips of paper (two to three inches wide) to go fully around the lazy Susan when taped together. Note: The strips will sit on top of the lazy Susan, not be taped to its sides.

Step 2: Draw a person or an animal performing an action. Break the single action up into about 12 consecutive motions, just as a cartoon animator would do. Use a black marker or bright colors.

Step 3: Using your craft knife, carefully make little slits above each drawing. The slits should be about 1/8 inch wide and 3/4 inch tall.

Step 4: Cut the bottom of your strips as shown, fold the tabs forward, and tape the ends of the strips together (with your drawings on the inside of the loop).

Step 5: Tape the loop to the lazy Susan and shine a flashlight onto the drawing directly opposite you. Look through the slit directly in front of you, give the lazy Susan a spin, and watch the action begin!

Suggestion: make different short clips of action-oriented Bible events.

ID TAGS

—Heather Down

For this game you will need at least five people. Ahead of time one person (who will not be playing) creates cards that each have a Bible character written on them. Each player gets one of these cards pinned to the back of their clothes with a safety pin. They are not allowed to look at the card; however, everyone else in the group can see it. The object of the game is to guess which character is on your back. You may ask people questions, but only questions that require a yes or no answer. When you have guessed your character, you can take the card off your back. The last person to guess his or her character makes the new cards for the next game.

Variation: Try other categories such as objects in a church, planets, famous Christian leaders—the possibilities are endless!

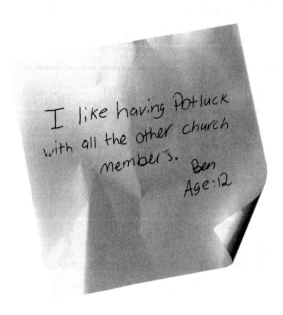

I like having Potluck with all the other church member's.
Ben
Age:12

Hidden Treasure

—Karen Pires

SABBATH ACTION BLAST

18

Geocaching is a worldwide treasure hunt with more than 95,000 caches (or treasures) hidden around the world. Someone hides a treasure and puts the coordinates on the Web. You look at www.geocaching.com to get the coordinates, and, using a GPS (Global Positioning System) unit,* go find the treasure. If you take a treasure, you are to replace it with something else. You might put in something that would remind the finder of their heavenly Father.

Virtual caches are something beautiful or interesting to look at. You might be surprised to find a swinging bridge, an Indian newspaper rock, or an old hidden cabin near your house that you never knew about!

Pathfinder leaders, check out the GeoTeaming link for some team ideas.

For worship you might want to read these verses: Matthew 13:44; Luke 12:33, 34. What treasures are these verses talking about? How do they compare to the treasures you found?

*Some geocaching does not require a GPS unit.

VEGETABLE Buddies

—Margaret Shauers

You will need:

- vegetables, such as carrots, potatoes, turnips, or beets
- yarn
- scraps of felt or fabric
- cotton swabs, toothpicks, pipe cleaners, cotton balls, corks, or anything else you have at home that might work
- thumbtacks
- white household glue
- markers

God's human creatures come in different colors, shapes, and sizes. Why not get together with your "different" friends and make a bunch of these zany vegetable buddies?

1. Look at the vegetables. Imagine a fun face for each one.
2. Start decorating a vegetable. You could thumbtack a piece of purple felt to a carrot for hair. Use thumbtacks to stick pipe cleaners in the sides for arms and legs. Cut felt bits to make a shirt, shoes, and mittens. Draw on a face with the marker. Or use tiny scraps of felt for eyes, nose, and a big tongue under a drawn smiling mouth. Give a turnip or a beet spider legs and a felt hat. Make a pig from a potato by adding toothpick legs and an old cork for a nose.
3. Keep a vegetable buddy for yourself. Then make one for someone you know who's sick or lonely. You're sure to make your friend smile and feel better.

I'VE GOT A SECRET

—Karen Troncale

Before playing, write everyone's names in a column on sheets of paper. You need one sheet for each person playing. Pass out blank paper and pencils. Tell each person to write down a "secret" about their lives that they think the others in the group don't know. Give a few examples before beginning, such as "I played a solo in band on Monday" or "I can do 25 push-ups."

Collect the "secrets." Pass out the papers with the names on them. Read each "secret" aloud. Choose a key word from the secret. Have everyone write the key word next to the name of the person they think wrote the secret.

After all the secrets have been read, read each one aloud again. The person who wrote it raises their hand. Each person circles that name if they guessed right, or crosses it off if they guessed wrong. Then everyone counts up the number of right guesses. The one with the most gets a small prize.

Sabbath is a great day to build relationships. This activity gives older people the chance to tell about something that happened to them a long time ago. It gives younger people the chance to be in the limelight for a moment. It's a fun way to learn about one another's lives!

Option: If you want, you could specify that the secret has to be about something nice you did for someone without their knowledge, or about something God has done for you.

Sabbath Upwords

—Ron Reese

Play the board game Upwords using only words you can find in the Bible. Each player can use a Bible and even a concordance if you have it. This game can be played with Scrabble, also.

Spiritual Food

—Priscilla Odinmah

Invite your friends and family to a "Spiritual Food" dinner!

Create a menu for each guest you want to invite. Make categories such as Appetizer, Entrée, Dessert, and Today's Special. But instead of real food items, in each section list Bible verses that you think apply to that category. Place about four to six verses in each section, except for Today's Special, in which you put one big, important, and unique verse.

Before your guests arrive, set the table with plates and place a Bible on each one, or tell your friends to bring their own Bibles. At the dinner everyone looks at the menu, chooses their "order," and then reads the verses they selected from the Bible. You can close with prayer.

If you like, you can also serve real food from Bible times or a simple snack! This is great for Friday sundown worship!

WREATH-MAKING

—Desiree Segna

A great indoor activity is wreath-making. Make a wreath for yourself and extras for friends and family.

Supplies can be purchased at a craft store (before Sabbath!), or collect your own materials on a Sabbath afternoon walk.

Evergreen Wreath

You will need:

- *wire frame*
- *evergreen boughs (cut your own or buy some at a tree lot)*
- *ribbon*
- *decorations, such as pinecones and berries*
- *wire*

Use boughs that are no longer than about six inches. Take three or four boughs in a bunch and tie them to the frame with wire. Continue in the same direction all the way around the rim. Then wire to the frame the decorations that you've chosen. Use the ribbon to tie a bow, and wire it to the frame.

Candy Wreath

You will need:

- *wire coat hanger (shaped into a circle) or embroidery hoop*
- *hard candy, such as bubble gum, Tootsie Rolls, etc.*
- *curly ribbon*
- *scissors or ribbon curler*

Cut strips of ribbon long enough to tie each piece of candy to the wreath frame. Tie the candy to your frame and then curl the ends of the ribbon. You may also cover the hook on the coat hanger with ribbon. If you wish, attach an inexpensive pair of scissors to the wreath with a piece of ribbon to cut off each piece of candy!

Friday Night Sabbath Party

—Lois Bailey

A party on Sabbath? Sure! Hold your Friday night Sabbath celebration in a parent's or church member's home. Start promptly at sundown with brief devotions. Then do a party-type Sabbath activity—for instance, play Bible charades (have a box of appropriate costumes, stuffed animals, etc., for props) or Bible Pictionary.

Then have supper. (If Sabbath starts late, you may want to do this first, but it's usually better to end with supper.) Be sure each person brings their prepared dish with them so that no one misses the party by being stuck in the kitchen! Keep the menu simple but interesting. Play Christian music CDs (preferably brought by the kids, but sponsors or parents should be prepared). End with a sharing prayer in a group.

Try doing this regularly, once a month or so. Invite your non-Adventist friends to share the joy of Sabbath!

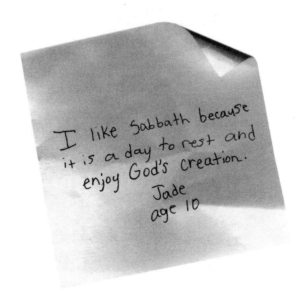

C'mon Dad, no videos?! Is it over yet?
we do?
WHAT T
HO HU
NE
cousin doesn't

CREATIVE CALENDAR

—Heather Down

Create your own wall calendar! Calendars are an ideal gift, too.

You can do this by hand, but there are some great computer programs that can help you. Illustrate each month with a picture (drawing or photo) of your choice. Here are some fun things to include:

- an inspirational quote or Bible verse for each month
- friends' and family members' birthdays
- *Guide* FACTory facts
- funny holidays (make up your own!)
- a monthly goal, such as reading the Bible daily, getting more exercise, or volunteering in the community

I like haveing time to go outside and enjoy nature.

Andrew
Age 13

Describo

—Adapted from *Non-Competitive Games*, Susan Butler, compiler (Bethany House Publishers, 1986).

Before play, have a nonparticipant prepare at least eight index cards that read "Category:_____." The blank space on each card should be filled in with a Sabbath-appropriate category or list (Bible or otherwise), such as Parts of the Body, Jesus' Disciples, Classmates' First Names, etc. Be creative with your categories! Below the category title on the card, write eight words belonging to that category.

The first player chooses a category card and tries to describe each word listed, using gestures and one-word clues (other than the actual word!). For example, clues for "hand" might be fingers, knuckles, fist, etc. The other members of the group call out their guesses until someone says the listed word. The goal is to try to get through the entire list on the card in one minute (or whatever other time you decide on beforehand).

Play continues with another person assuming the role of clue-giver and choosing another category card.

Alpha-speak Improv

—Heather Down

Pick two actors to be two Bible characters. They must hold a conversation, alternating sentences back and forth in character, starting each new sentence with the next letter of the alphabet. To make it more fun, add a time challenge, and see if they can go through the entire alphabet beating the clock!

SABBATH ACTION BLAST
28

TALKING BOOKS

—Violet Nesdoly

You will need:
- *a picture storybook (choose one appropriate for Sabbath)*
- *a cassette tape recorder*
- *a blank cassette tape*
- *a bell or other soundmaker to tell when to turn the page*

Little kids often like to hear the same story over and over. But the older people who read to them usually don't enjoy it so much! Here's a solution: make a storybook tape for a younger brother, sister, or friend. Then they can listen as often as they want.

1. Read the story out loud once for practice.
2. Put the blank tape into the cassette recorder and begin the recording by giving the story's title and author. Also tell the listener what sound you will make to tell them it's time to turn the page.
3. Read the story into the recorder microphone, remembering to play the page-turn sound each time you turn the page.

Tip: Bring the book and tape along to entertain the children at your next babysitting job. They make great outreach gifts, too!

Quad Collect
—Heather Down

Create a set of 52 game cards: 13 categories with four cards each. You can use premade blank cards or cut your own out of card stock. Use such categories as Bible people, stories, or objects; Adventist pioneers, missionaries, or preachers; nature objects. Illustrate the cards and list the category on each, plus the other items in the category.

Each player receives five cards. Try to collect complete categories by asking another player for a specific card that goes with ones you already have. If they have the card, they give it to you, and you take another turn. If they don't have the requested card, you must draw one from the remaining cards, and the next player takes a turn. The person with the most complete categories wins.

33

SAB-2

PROGRESSIVE LUNCH

—Brenda Segna

Find several families willing to host your junior or earliteen class for Sabbath lunch. Each home provides only part of the lunch, and the class goes from house to house.

Here's one way to divide it up:

1. First home—chips and salsa; juice
2. Second home—soup and salad
3. Third home—main course
4. Fourth home—dessert and, depending on the time, sundown worship
5. Fifth home—popcorn and videos

You'll have fun getting better acquainted with people in your church.

COMPASS HUNT

—Andrew Roderick

You will need:
- *two compasses*
- *12 sheets of paper (six per group)*
- *two pencils or pens*
- *a large outdoor area*

Divide into two groups, each having a compass and six sheets of paper. Decide where each group will start the hike. Each group chooses six stopping points along the hike. With the help of the compass, keep track of how many paces and what direction you take to reach each stop. At each stop, hide a clue giving directions to the next stop (kind of like a treasure hunt).

When each group has created all their clues, come back to the start. Then have the groups switch clues with each other for finding the first stop. Using your compass and the clues, follow their directions until you find them all. The first group that gets back is the winner.

Optional ending: Hide a nature item at the last stop.

C'mon Dad, no videos?! Is it over yet?

What th

Ho hu

we do?

cousin doesn't

Ne

BOXES OF FUN

—Rachel Whitaker

Do you love getting mail? Imagine how much you'd look forward to letters and packages if you were a mission kid living overseas. Sending a care package is a great way to brighten a missionary's day.

1. Think of things a kid far from home might enjoy: books, games, nonperishable food, a small toy. Be creative!
2. Write a note to say hello and share news or introduce yourself. You might include photos or an encouraging Bible verse.
3. Pack everything carefully—try to make your package indestructible! Small packages often survive better than large ones.

If you don't know any missionaries, here are some ways to find them.

• Contact one of these associate secretaries of the General Conference of Seventh-day Adventists: Douglas Clayville (ClayvilleD@gc.adventist.org), Agustin Galicia (GaliciaA@gc.adventist.org), Larry Evans (EvansL@gc.adventist.org). You can also reach them through the GC's main number: 301-680-6000.
• Visit Adventist Frontier Missions at www.afmonline.org. Click on "Missionaries." Each family's page has a "How You Can Help" section that lists things they'd like and tells how to ship packages to them.

You could also choose a military serviceperson, a student at boarding school, or even a friend who's moved away.

Wacky Words

—Janelle Wahlman

Ahead of time, the leader selects a list of Bible words and definitions, using a Bible encyclopedia or Bible dictionary. The leader chooses three people to be on the Wacky Word team and divides the rest into teams of two to eight players. The leader reads the first word aloud. Then each person on the Wacky Word team writes a definition for the word on a slip of paper. It may be what they think the word really means, or something that sounds logical. The leader writes the correct definition on a slip of paper. All definitions are then passed to the leader, who reads the four definitions aloud. Each team selects the definition they think is correct, and each team with the correct answer scores one point. More than one team may have the correct answer.

Here are some words from the King James Version to get you started. Definitions for these and many other Bible words can be found in the Christian Answers WebBible Encyclopedia (www.christiananswers.net/dictionary/home.html).

ALMUG	(1 Kings 10:11)	a stick of sandalwood
BUZI	(Ezekiel 1:3)	Ezekiel's father
CHRYSOPRASUS	(Revelation 21:20)	a greenish-golden stone
FIRKIN	(John 2:6)	a measure for liquids
GOB	(2 Samuel 21:18, 19)	site of battles with the Philistines
IIM	(Numbers 33:45)	place Israel camped in the wilderness
JACINTH	(Revelation 21:20)	deep-purple flower or stone
LIGNALOES	(Numbers 24:6)	Oriental perfume or tree
MINCING	(Isaiah 3:16)	taking short, quick steps
ONYCHA	(Exodus 30:34)	an ingredient for incense
PRAETORIUM	(Mark 15:16)	the governor's house
SOP	(John 13:26)	a piece of bread
TRACHONITIS	(Luke 3:1)	a rugged region east of Jordan
ZAMZUMMIMS	(Deuteronomy 2:20)	a race of giants

CUSTOM MEMORY VERSE "DECK"

—Randy Fishell

Watch your friends' mouths drop open when you begin recalling memory verses like an Olympic champion! Here's a great way to get you moving in that direction.

Get some 3" x 5" index cards. Choose a Bible verse that you want to memorize and write it on one side of a card. On the other side of the card, using thin, colored markers or your preferred choice of drawing utensil(s), draw a picture (either realistic or silly) to help trigger the verse in your mind (see example below).

Create several cards using different verses and pictures. Then try to recite each verse simply by looking at that verse's picture. Get some friends to do this project with you, and you can quiz each other. You can even make it into a simple game and keep score.

Over time you will be surprised how many verses you can recall using this method.

Example:

"Come, follow me," Jesus said, "and I will make you fishers of men" (Matthew 4:19).

ANSWERED PRAYER TALK SHOW

—Jim McDevitt

Has anyone you know experienced an answer to prayer or a dramatic evidence of God's protection? Here's a fun way to find out.

For family worship or with a group of kids and adults, ask each person to think of an example of God's intervention that they've experienced personally. Pretend you are the host of a TV talk show. (You can make up a name for your show and even create a stage if you wish!) Invite each "guest" to come up, and interview them about their answered prayer or miracle story. Besides having them tell their story, you could ask what they learned about God during that time, what advice they have about prayer, or what scriptures relate to their experience.

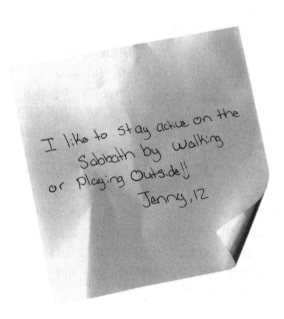

I like to stay active on the Sabbath by walking or playing outside!!
Jenny, 12

Bible Dash

—Carly Sim

Choose one leader who is not on either team. Before the game, the leader makes a list of Bible verses containing a word that is drawable, and writes down how many words from the beginning that word is. (The leader should be sure to write down the answer for each verse!)

Divide players into two teams. You will need at least three or four people on each team to make it work right, but this game can be played with as many people as you want, as long as the teams are even. It is more fun the more people you have.

Have each team sit in chairs placed in two single-file lines. Give the last person in line on both teams a Bible.

The leader tells a verse and says how many words from the beginning. For example, "Exodus 40:25, fifth word from the beginning." The person holding the Bible will then look up the verse and find the chosen word. (In the example, the word is "lamps.") They whisper that word to the person in front of them, and that person will whisper it to the person in front of them, and so on.

As soon as the person in the very front hears the word, they will run up to a whiteboard, chalkboard, or table with paper for each team. They will then draw that object, and the leader should be able to tell what it is. As soon as they're done, they will run back to their seat and sit down. Whoever sits first will earn a point for their team.

The whole line will move up, so the person who just drew goes to the back to look up the next verse. This game can be played as long as desired, and whichever team gets the most points wins.

This game is fun because it's a mixture of Telephone and Pictionary. Sometimes the drawings will end up being nothing like what was mentioned in the verse.

BROWN BAG TALES

—Randy Fishell

Jesus often used stories to share spiritual truths, and so can you!

Have each participant place about a dozen random items in a paper bag. Include a wide range of items, such as a wooden match, a sock, a pencil, a Lego block, etc.

Swap bags with someone else and take no more than five minutes to create a spiritually meaningful story that involves all of the items in the bag. Take turns telling the stories, holding up each item as you come to it in the story line.

Option: Use the items symbolically or as a "sounds like" word. Example (using the items mentioned above): "Nikki cried out, 'Sergio, you think I'm no match for you. But you'd better Lego of my jacket or I'm gonna sock you!' Suddenly she stopped and thought . . ."

Have fun with your one-of-a-kind tale-spinning!

WAGGING TAILS

—Rachel Whitaker

If you love animals but don't have pets of your own, why not adopt one for an hour or two?

Call your local animal shelter and see if they need volunteers to walk dogs and play with the animals. (You'll probably need an adult with you. And not all shelters allow kids to volunteer.)

Ask your neighbors who have dogs if they'd like you to walk their pet—for free, of course!

WAGGING TAILS CONTINUED

These are great ways to serve, connect with God's creation, and make new friends, including four-footed pals who will give you lots of love in return. That means you'll celebrate at least three of the special reasons God gave us the Sabbath!

SING A NEW SONG

—Melanie Scherencel Bockmann

Do this activity with other kids or a mix of kids and adults.

Choose an easy tune, such as "Oh, Fill It Up," and have each participant make up a verse (you may want to have paper and pencils handy) about a Bible character chosen by another person. For instance, one person may say, "Saul of Tarsus," and the next singer would have to make up a verse about Saul, such as:

Saul of Tarsus was a scary guy
Who wouldn't listen at all.
But after he got knocked off his horse,
He straightened up and heeded God's call.

The versemaker then gets to choose a Bible character for the next person to sing about. This activity is fun and produces laughs until the voices (or the imaginations) wear out.

NOT-THE-SAME NAME GAME

—Ron Reese

In this game, being different is good!

Give a piece of paper to each player. At the top of the page, going across, write four categories, such as Bible women, Bible cities, Bible animals, and Bible plants.

Play is similar to the game Balderdash. For the first round, each player has to think of an item for each category and write it in the appropriate column.

To figure the score, each player reads their first answer. If no one else thought of the same answer as you, you get a point for each person playing. For instance, if there are five people in the game, and no one has the same Bible woman as you, then you would get five points. Subtract one point for each player who chose the same person. So if two players choose the same person, they each get three points. If everyone thought of the same person, then you all get a zero for that item.

Follow the same procedure for the other categories in the first round.

The game continues for 10 rounds.

You can also use other categories from the Bible, nature, church history, and other Sabbath-appropriate topics. Examples include miracles of the Bible, world religions and denominations, animals that live in the water, etc.

DRAW THE PROVERB

—Lynette Allcock

You don't have to be a master artist to enjoy this fun activity!

Simply pick a proverb and illustrate it—cartoon-style is a good choice.

Here are a few ideas to get you started: Proverbs 14:31; 17:9; 20:11. Or, for a humorous approach, try verses such as Proverbs 17:1, 12, 14; 19:24; 20:17.

After you've done several illustrations, you could make a book from your best work and give it to a friend as a great God-centered gift!

QUESTION TOSS

—Lance Downing

In this game you have fun with people while learning about the Bible.

Everyone playing stands in a circle. One person holds a ball. Whoever has the ball asks a Bible question that he or she knows the answer to and then quickly tosses the ball randomly to someone in the circle. If they drop the ball or answer incorrectly, they are out of the game. If they catch the ball and get the question right, however, they yell out a question and randomly toss the ball. Play till only one person is left.

Option: use a Frisbee instead of a ball.

No-Camera Silent Movie

—Randy Fishell

Create a silent film effect without using a movie camera!

You will need:
- *three flashlights*
- *optional: white bedsheet*

Write or choose a Sabbath-appropriate story as the basis of your "movie." Assign parts for actors and actresses to act out. (Have them wear black and white clothes if possible.)

Tape the bed-sheet to a wall (or use the wall itself if it is white). This will serve as the movie screen. Have participants take their places in front of the "screen," and turn out all the lights. Important: For the best effect, the area should be totally dark.

To create the movie effect, have three people turn on the flashlights, aim them at the movie screen, and shake them up and down very quickly. (The flashlights should be held about six to 10 feet away from the screen.) As the story is read aloud by a narrator, participants act out the story. You will be surprised how much this looks like an old-time movie!

c'mon Dad, no videos?!
What'll we do?
Is it over yet?
HO HU
WHAT T
NE
cousin doesn't

OVER THE SEA

—Adapted from Vernon Howard,
Handbook of Bible Games (Zondervan, 1953).

For this fun game someone needs to write several relatively well-known countries on slips of paper, which are then placed in a bowl or hat. The first player draws a slip and announces, "I'm going as a missionary to . . . " Instead of saying the name of the country, the player must pantomime (act out) and use gestures to reveal the country. For example, a player might reveal Australia by imitating a kangaroo and throwing a boomerang. Players attempt to guess what country is being represented. Play continues with the person who guessed correctly pantomiming their country. If no one guesses correctly within a given amount of time, the player may then provide spoken clues. Play continues until all the slips have been used.

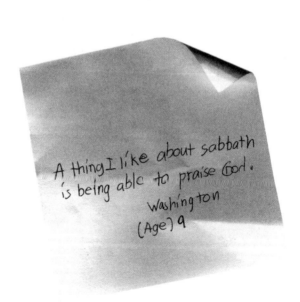

A thing I like about sabbath is being able to praise God.
Washington
(Age) 9

TREASURE HUNT

—Melanie Scherencel Bockmann

This tried-and-true fun activity can be done indoors or outdoors. You can set it up for your friends or younger siblings. Or your parents could create one for all the kids! The "treasure" can be something simple, such as dessert, because the fun part is the hunt!

The "huntmaster" creates a set of 10 or more clues based on Bible texts, which he or she hides throughout the house or yard. The clue is simply a Bible text, such as Psalm 119:105. When the hunters look it up in the Bible, they find: "Your word is a lamp to my feet and a light for my path" (NIV). The second clue may be hidden under a lamp and may be the text 1 Samuel 28:23: "He refused and said, 'I will not eat.' But his men joined the woman in urging him, and he listened to them. He got up from the ground and sat on the couch" (NIV). The next clue may be hidden in or under the couch.

This hunt gives you a reason to dig through the Bible and a chance to be creative. The possibilities are as endless as the imagination. For instance, if the family owns a Dodge Caravan, Genesis 37:25 might be a fun one: "As they sat down to eat their meal, they looked up and saw a caravan . . ." (NIV). The next clue could be in the vehicle's glove compartment.

This is a time-consuming activity, and you can spend a good amount of your Sabbath afternoon with this treasure hunt.

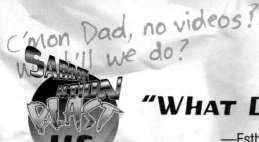

"WHAT Did You See?"

—Esther Corina Gow-Lee

One person goes out of the room, and the rest decide on a Bible story.

After they decide, person A walks back into the room and says, "Nora, what did you see?"

Let's say they decided on Moses crossing the Red Sea. Nora comes up with something that she might have seen if she had been there, such as "I saw a large body of water."

Person A tries to guess the story. If the guess is wrong, he/she asks the next player, "Jamie, what did you see?"

Jamie replies, "Lots of red."

The game keeps going until person A finally guesses the story. Then the person who gave the last clue trades places with person A. To make it easier and more fun, use all of the senses, such as smell and hearing. (For instance, you could say you smelled a lot of salt.)

BALLOON LAUNCH

—Heather Shreve

At a park, send up helium balloons with your church's name and address attached, along with a Bible quote or small tract.

Be sure to use biodegradable balloons (available at party supply stores) to avoid creating litter that could harm wildlife.

Visit www.newlifeministries-nlm.org/ideas/balloon.htm for ideas on making this a fun activity for your whole church!

Situation Skits

—Lois Bailey

48

On individual pieces of paper, write brief descriptions of situations that a young person might face. For example: "A new kid with a physical disability comes to your school. Some students begin picking on him." Or "A mother is cleaning and discovers drugs in her daughter's room. When the daughter returns home, the mother confronts her."

Form small groups. Each group picks a situation, and the members have three to five minutes to discuss possible outcomes before acting out their situation for everyone else. You can have costumes and props available.

After each skit, discuss what happened and how a Christian should react in this situation. You may wish to find Bible texts ahead of time that apply to each situation.

A "cast party" with treats or a simple supper is a great ending!

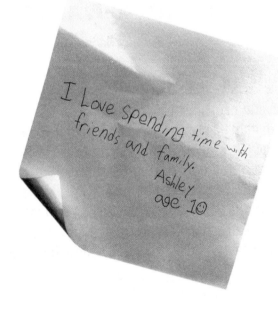

I Love spending time with friends and family.
Ashley
age 10

EARS TO HEAR

—Hannah Chandler

Each participant picks a partner. One person without a partner makes an obstacle course out of chairs and other objects (indoors or outdoors). Blindfold one person from each pair and spin them around. Then the other partner must lead the blindfolded person through the course by giving instructions, such as "Turn left," "Crawl under this," or "Step over that." To make it harder, you can have special instructions, such as "Crawl on your stomach for four feet; then jump sideways in small bounces."

Before or after this activity, have a worshipful discussion about "hearing" God's voice and heeding His instructions.

CLAP-A-NAME

—Samuel Nadarajan

You'll need several people to play this funny game. First, come up with a clapping rhythm that lasts somewhere around 10 to 12 seconds.

Then have one player think of a Bible name. While everyone does the clapping rhythm, the next person has to think of another Bible name that starts with the last letter of the previous name. As soon as the player says a name, start the rhythm over and go to the next person. Example: Obadiah—Hannah—Haman—Nebuchadnezzar, etc.

The player who cannot think of a name before the rhythm is done is out of the game. No name can be mentioned twice. The last player still in the game wins.

You can also use other Sabbath-appropriate categories, such as animals, plants, things in a church, etc.

Reworked Word Balloons

This is a fun way to put a faith-building twist on the Sunday comics.

Choose a comic strip and cover the words in the word balloons with typewriter correction fluid. Or you may scan the comics and remove the words digitally.

Replace the words with local names, places, events, etc. *The new story line should have a spiritual point.* You may wish to use family or church members' names in the story line. If you want to add the words digitally, consider using the typeface Comic Sans. (Be sure and print out your work when you're finished.)

If you prefer, draw your own comic and story line. Either way, share the end product with your family, friends, and church family!

FALSE PROPHETS

—Wam Akakulu

A prophet is a person who is called by God to speak for Him to His people. But Jesus warned us that some people will claim to speak for God while actually speaking Satan's lies. Knowing God's Word is essential for recognizing the truth!

In this game you will need two groups, the prophets and the people of God. The prophets choose one or more members of their group to be false prophets, without letting the people of God know who's who. Then the people of God are to guess which prophets are from God and which are not, based on whether their statements agree with the Bible. The prophets must take turns speaking. A prophet of God might say something such as "You must believe in the Lord Jesus Christ, and you will be saved." A false prophet would say something such as "Only Jesus and the Father know when Jesus is coming." (Only the Father knows, according to Matthew 24:36.) Both teams may use Bibles to figure out true and false statements.

When the people of God guess right, they get one point. But if they guess wrong, the prophets get one point. You can play until the people of God know who all the false prophets are.

FLIP 'EM OVER

—Ron Clark

Make your own memory game! Cut poster board into uniform squares. Then look through magazines and cut out Sabbath-appropriate pictures of matching items—anything from the map off the back of a Sabbath school quarterly to pictures from a Pathfinder Camporee. You can use two identical pictures or cut one picture into two halves. Glue the pictures onto the squares. Make at least 10 pairs of cards.

To play, place the cards facedown in rows. Players take turns flipping over two cards, looking for a matching set. When a match is made, that player gets another turn. The person to collect the most pairs wins.

Jeffrey
One thing that I like
to do is go on a
walk and look at nature.
Age, 13

WRITE TURNS

—Karolina K. Shafar

Have everyone in the family get a notebook to use as a journal. You can purchase a blank book that you like, or you can decorate a plain notebook yourself.

On Sabbath, gather everyone in a comfortable spot at home. Turn off any distractions, such as the TV and radio. Each person writes down in their journal any problems or feelings that they have had during the week, and the way they dealt with them.

Then have each person read something they wrote. Discuss whether they dealt with the problem or feeling the way Jesus would. Offer suggestions for the best ways to deal with the situation next time. Each person can also make specific goals for being more like Jesus during the coming week.

HALF WORDS

—Callum Hughes

Each player for this Bible game should have a pen or pencil and several pieces of lined paper. Choose a person to write a Bible name, using all capital letters. That person then folds the paper so only half of the word can be seen, and shows it to the group. (Decide ahead of time whether they should show the top half, the bottom half, the beginning half, or the ending half.) The person who guesses the name gets to write the next Bible name. If no one gets it right, the writer chooses another person to write.

Try the same activity using a variety of drawings and photos!

GARDEN STEPPING-STONES

—Kay Rizzo

56

*C*ast a lasting memento of God's creation!

You will need:
- bag of ready-mixed quick-drying concrete
- several small pebbles to surround design
- plastic plant saucers
- cooking spray
- items to embed or imprint in concrete, such as:
  - seashells—can be purchased at craft store during non-Sabbath hours
  - stones—polished or regular (can be purchased at craft store)
  - handprint and name
  - plastic fruit—imprint images of the fruit; then carve names of fruit of the Spirit found in Galatians 5:22, 23
  - leaves—draw around leaves onto cardboard, cut them out, and use as a pattern to imprint into cement

Directions:
1. Plan the stepping-stone design on paper.
2. Spray inside surfaces of plant saucers with cooking spray to make removal of set concrete easier.
3. Mix concrete as directed by manufacturer and pour it into the prepared plant saucers. (The thicker the concrete in the mold, the stronger the finished stone will be.)
4. Decorate stepping-stones as desired.
5. Allow concrete to set; then remove finished stones from plant saucers.
6. Display your stepping-stones outdoors (they are best used for decoration rather than for walking on).

Code Relay

—Samuel Nadarajan

Create several different codes and write them on a big sheet of paper so that everyone can see. (Examples: A=1, B=2, C=3; or A=Z, B=Y, C=X; etc.) Do not write out the entire code, however. Players must figure this out.

Divide into teams with no more than four players per team. Have all the teams line up. Players must be spaced far enough apart so that they can't see each other's writing. A person who isn't playing will choose one of the codes listed and write a Bible phrase in that code. Then the person will hand the coded phrase to the first player on each team.

Example:
  7-15-4 9-19 12-15-22-5   (God is love)

The first player then decodes it and converts the same phrase into a different code listed. In the example, the coded phrase would be TLW RH OLEV.

The player then passes the new code to the next player, who decodes it and converts it into a different code listed, and so on. (No talking allowed!) The team that finishes first and has carried the message accurately to the end wins.

Option: For a faster-paced game, have every player come up with their own phrase. Everyone converts it to code at the same time and passes it to the next player in line to decode.

God's Scrapbook

—Rachel Whitaker

Someone once suggested that we can think of the Bible as "God's journal of the things important to Him." Imagine what it would be like if God had given us the Bible as a scrapbook with photos, news clippings, and other memories of His family on earth, along with His letters to them and His plans for their future. Then use your creativity to make up some pages from God's scrapbook!

For instance, some pages of God's scrapbook might include "photos of My best friends." Draw pictures of Bible heroes and famous Christians and add a caption telling what they've done for God. Don't forget to include yourself and maybe some people from your church! Another page might be "My Son—I'm so proud of Him." Here you'd include stories and pictures from Jesus' life on earth. Other pages could include "My best advice for life" and "snapshots of the home I'm building for you in heaven."

Sharing God's Word

—Sarah Nadarajan

Here's a great outreach project: take your *Guide* and make a Sabbath afternoon church service out of it. With your family or friends, make and decorate handbills announcing your program. Pass them out and invite your friends or neighborhood kids over. Present your church service to them, and make it really fun!

For example, use the lesson study as the sermon. Use the stories and games from *Guide* to make the service even better! Throw in a *Sabbath Action Blast* idea as a fun activity.

c'mon Dad, no videos?!
what'll we do?
Is it over yet?

WHAT TI

HO HU

NE

cousin doesn't

SABBATH ACTION BLAST

60

BiblE BasEbALL

—Jordan Stolz

First you need Bible trivia cards (use cards from another game or make up your own questions). Then get pillows or other soft things to use as bases and set them up as a diamond in your living room. (You can also play outside.)

Divide into two teams. The team asking the questions decides, based on the difficulty, if the question is a "single," "double," "triple," or "home run." If you answer the question correctly, move that number of bases. If you answer wrong, you're "out"! Each team gets three "outs" per inning.

You don't have to keep score. Just play for the fun of it!

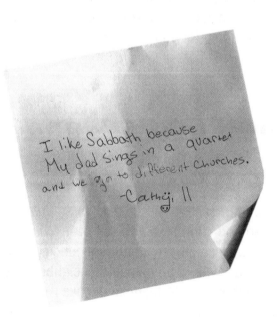

I like Sabbath because
My dad sings in a quartet
and we go to different Churches.
—Cathy, 11

PARENT DETECTIVES

—Doris Hier

61

Sometimes it's hard to think of your parents as once being your age with some of the same problems you face. How much do you know about their lives when they were growing up?

Answer the following about your parent or parents:

1. Name a pet your parent had as a child.
2. What kind of student was your parent?
3. What was their favorite fun activity?
4. Who was your parent's best friend?
5. What was their favorite food?
6. Did your parent get allowances? If so, how much?
7. Who were their role models or heroes at the time?
8. What makes your parent most proud of you?
9. What do you do that annoys them the most?
10. In what ways are you like them when they were growing up?
11. How are you different?
12. What things do you have that they did not have?

Now ask your parent or parents the questions, and see if you guessed their answers!

C'mon Dad, no videos?!
we do?
Is it over yet?
WHAT T
cousin doesn't
HO HU
NE

BiBLe SpeLLiNG Bee

SABBATH ACTION BLAST 62

—Stephanie Hubbard

Before playing this game, you will need to write out a list of words from the Bible and put them in columns of easy, medium, and hard. Now you can play!

Divide into two teams, plus a moderator to read the words. The moderator reads a word to a player on the first team. If that person doesn't spell the word correctly, then the other side gets a chance to spell it. Work from easy to hard on the word list. Have the moderator keep track of points.

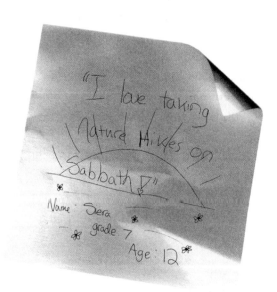

"I love taking Nature Hikes on Sabbath!"

Name: Sera
grade 7
Age: 12

LAST TO FALL

—Samuel Nadarajan

SABBATH ACTION BLAST

63

You will need:

- *toothpicks*
- *glue (wood glue is best, since it dries quickly)*
- *some form of weight (not more than one to two pounds)*

Divide the participants into groups of two or three. Give each group an equal amount of toothpicks and glue. Tell them that they have to build a structure that is not longer than one foot and not wider than one foot. It doesn't matter how high they make it. Their goal is to make a very strong structure that can hold a lot of weight. Give them about one to two hours for brainstorming, building, and drying.

When the structures are completely dry, take weights (books, common household items, small weights, or anything else that is heavy) and slowly place them one by one on top of the structure. Keep going until the structure falls or breaks. Which one held the most weight?

After testing the structures, ask each group what their building strategy was. Discuss how this relates to the way God created our bodies, using verses such as Genesis 1:27; Psalm 139:14-16; 1 Corinthians 3:16, 17. God designed each of our bodies to be strong, but defiling our bodies (through smoking, drugs, or stimulants) can cause them to become weak. Challenge participants to keep their bodies strong!

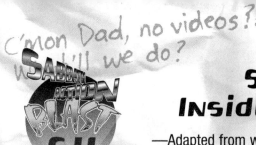

SEEING INSIDE YOUR EYE

—Adapted from www.exploratorium.edu/snacks

SABBATH ACTION BLAST 64

The retina is the membrane at the back of your eye that senses the images coming in. You can actually look at your own retina—or at least the blood vessels in it.

You will need:

- *a small, dim flashlight, such as a Mini Maglite® or penlight*
- *a sheet of black paper*
- *a completely dark room*

In the dark room, stare straight ahead at the black paper from a few inches away. Point the flashlight straight up and hold it a half inch or less in front of and slightly below the center of one eye. Move the light slowly from side to side a short distance (a quarter inch). Keep doing this for about 20 seconds. You should begin to see a pattern that looks like the branches of a tree. (If this doesn't work, experiment with different lights.)

What you see is the network of arteries and veins that supply blood to your retina. The blood vessels are slightly in front of the retina, so the light casts their shadow on the retina. Normally you don't see the network because it never changes, and your eye ignores unchanging images. But when you move the flashlight, the shadow moves, and you can see it!

BIBLE WHEEL OF FORTUNE

—Timothy Yun

This game is like Wheel of Fortune. All you need is a whiteboard and markers.

Have the host choose a phrase from the Bible or other Sabbath-appropriate source. Players can be told the topic, such as Bible characters, places, etc.

Draw one blank space for each of the phrase's letters. Leave an empty space between words. The first player calls out a consonant. If the letter is contained in the phrase, the host writes it in the appropriate blank, and that player continues. The player receives one point for each time the letter appears. If the letter is not contained in the phrase, play moves to the next player.

Players may "buy" vowels at an appropriate "cost" in points.

The first player (or team) to guess the phrase wins that round. The player with the most points at the end of play is the winner.

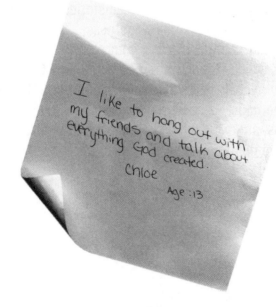

I like to hang out with my friends and talk about everything God created.

Chloe
Age :13

BiBLE-TiME CAMPOUT

—Rachel Whitaker

Would you like to experience a holiday that Jesus and other Bible characters celebrated? In Leviticus 23:33-43 God told the Israelites to live in temporary "booths" for seven days to remember their years of camping in the wilderness. Today this holiday is called Sukkot, or the Feast of Tabernacles, and begins at sundown on the fifth day after Yom Kippur. Check a calendar to find out which day Sukkot is celebrated this year. You can enjoy this spiritual celebration with your family and friends.

First, build your outdoor shelter (called a sukkah, pronounced SOOK-uh). Use as many natural materials as possible to construct and cover it—wood, tree branches, cornstalks, and other plants. You can decorate it with flowers, vegetables, dried grasses, etc.

Here are some fun things to do in your sukkah, especially on Sabbath:

• Eat meals together as a family.

• Have family worship each day. Read stories of events that happened to the Israelites in the wilderness.

• If the weather is good, sleep in your sukkah overnight.

During this holiday the Jews remembered how God had led and protected them in their history. Now is a good time to learn about your spiritual heritage. Ask older family members to tell how they became Christians, and have them share stories of times God provided for them or gave them guidance.

CONCERT FOR CHRIST

—Sarah Nadarajan

61

Do you enjoy singing or playing an instrument? Use the gift of music to help reach others and invite them to make a commitment to Christ.

Plan a concert and invite friends, family, church members, and non-Adventists. If you wish, ask friends who like to sing or play to help present the music.

Choose songs that will move the hearts of those you invite toward God. Between the songs, tell your audience why you chose those songs and what they mean to you. For example, you might sing "Jesus Loves Me" and tell the story of its author. Include your testimony as well—tell them how God has led in your life.

At the end of the concert, make an altar call asking people to accept Jesus as their personal Savior. After the concert, provide refreshments, and take time to get to know your guests better. As they leave, give them a *Guide*, and in that *Guide* put a handbill inviting them to visit your church or to meet your local pastor.

SAB-3

FRONT OR BACK

*H*ere's a simple game that's surprisingly engaging!

Write the following categories on slips of paper: Bible Foods, Things in Outer Space, Classmate's First Names, Trees, Old Testament Characters, Sea Life, Animals, Birds, Vegetables, Fruits, New Testament Characters, Protestant Reformers, Hymn Titles, Relative's Names. (You may add as many categories as you wish.) Fold the slips in half and place them in a bowl.

A random word from the Bible is written down to begin play. The person to the left of the person who wrote this word calls out "Front" or "Back" and then rolls a die (or other preferred device).

The player then counts in from the front or the back (depending on what they chose) of the written word the number of letters they rolled on the die. Example—Word: Nebuchadnezzar; die roll, 5; chosen direction, front. Counting in five letters from the front of Nebuchadnezzar results in the letter C.

Next, the player chooses a random category from the category bowl. His or her answer must begin with the letter their die has pointed to. In the example, their letter would be C. If the player happened to draw the category Fruits, they might answer "cantaloupe." Maximum stall time is 30 seconds. Scoring: 1 point for each letter.

The most recent player's word now becomes the word the next player must base his or her answer upon. Play proceeds to the left. Play ends when a prearranged winning score level is reached.

Option: If a player cannot think of a word, others may step in. The person with the highest-scoring word wins the points.

FREEZE-FRAME GUESSING GAME

—Randy Fishell

Here's a fun and frequently funny activity that's especially good for a larger group.

Divide into groups of two to four. Each group chooses a Bible or other Sabbath-appropriate scene to depict. The first group forms themselves into a freeze-frame shot of their chosen scene, and then others have to guess what's being depicted. The next group then depicts their scene, and so forth.

Examples of scenes include Abraham's servant meeting Rebekah at the well; David cutting off part of King Saul's garment; Paul being let down over the wall of Damascus in a basket. (Remember—no moving!) Try some unusual scenes to keep things interesting!

Creating the scene behind a curtain or bedsheet and then revealing the scene with a flourish adds a fun twist to this activity.

Options: incorporate simple props into the scene; use people to form inanimate objects.

Question: what "scene" from your life would you like to have someone depict someday?

C'mon Dad, no videos?! What'll we do? Is it over yet? WHAT T

HO HU

NE

cousin doesn't

SABBATH ACTION BLAST 10

SAY THANKS

—Melanie Scherencel Bockmann

*F*or this activity you need a set of note cards (or make your own cards), a church directory, and a book of stamps. Pick a few names from the church directory, such as someone who has done special music for church, a Sabbath school teacher, a greeter, the person who types the bulletin, or even someone who is sick and missed church. Write notes of appreciation, thanking these people for what they do. The notes don't have to be long—even a couple of sincere lines can create "warm fuzzies" in the person who receives them and the person who writes them!

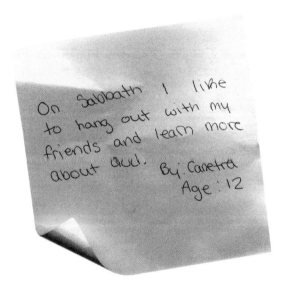

On Sabbath I like to hang out with my friends and learn more about God. By: Canetra Age: 12

Gifts From God

—Suvi Anderson

A greeting card with a surprise a day for a whole week tells others how much you and God love them!

Step 1: Fold two pieces of thick paper in half together to make a four-page booklet. Draw a three-quarter-inch border on the front.

Step 2: On a third sheet, draw a 1¼-inch square with a tab sticking out halfway down one side *(see illustration).* Cut out this template and lightly trace it seven times, randomly arranged, inside the border.

Step 3: Separate the folded sheets and carefully cut each square on the tabbed and two adjoining sides so that it folds back as a window.

Step 4: Lay the window sheet and the other folded sheet flat and paste them together—but don't glue the windows shut!

Step 5: Close the windows. Fold back each tab and cut a slit in the inside layer along the tab's folded edge. (The tab will slip into the slit to hold the window shut.)

Step 6: Write the numbers 1 to 7 on the windows (for the days of the week on which the person is supposed to open the windows).

Step 7: Inside each window, write a gift from God, such as "animals" or "love," and draw its picture above it. Write "You!" in the last window and draw a picture of the person you are giving the card to.

Step 8: Write "Gifts From God" along the top of your card, decorate it, and write a greeting inside. Tuck in the tabs and send it off!

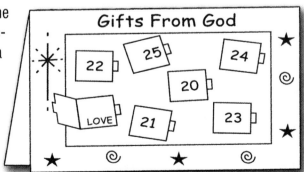

CATEGORY CHALLENGE

—Sarah Nadarajan

SABBATH ACTION BLAST 12

You'll need four or more players for this game. Have an adult think of categories in the Bible, such as weapons, pairs in the New Testament, tribes of Israel, etc. They should then write each category at the top of a 4" x 6" card, and below write 10 things that relate to the category. (You can also use other Sabbath-honoring categories, such as nature.)

Divide into teams of two. Have the adult choose a category card and read the selected category to the first team. Players have three minutes to guess all 10 words on the front side of the card. Each correct word is worth four points. Words not listed receive no points, even if they fit the category. For example, if the category is weapons and someone yells out "sling" but it is not on the card, they will not get points.

The next team then tries a different category. The team with the most points wins!

COAT OF ARMS

—Kim Kasch

This shield with a personalized coat of arms makes a great gift to remind a friend of the "armor of God" (Ephesians 6:10-17). Or work with your family members to create your own family crest.

Cut out the shape of a shield from a 12" x 24" piece of cardboard. Wrap it in duct tape until it is completely covered. This will give the shield the look of armor and stiffen it. Divide the shield into four quadrants.

Here are some things you can put on the shield:

- Pictures that reflect the history behind the person's family name. For example, the name Kasch is German, so you could use a German flag.
- Pictures that reflect your friend's personality or interests: skating, basketball, flowers, guitar.
- Pictures that represent good qualities your friend has or goals you encourage them to aspire to, such as a book for knowledge or a crown for eternal life.
- A phrase or Bible text as a motto, such as "Soldier for God" or "Never Give Up."

Glue one picture into each of the four quadrants, leaving a rim of silver duct tape showing around the edges. Add the person's family name. After completing the design, cover the entire shield with clear tape, or paint a mixture of one part water to two parts Elmer's glue over the front of the shield to protect the pictures.

To create a handle, cover a scrap piece of cardboard with duct tape and tape it to the back of the shield.

C'mon Dad, no videos?! Is it over yet? WHAT T,

u Sah'll we do? HO HU

cousin doesn't NE

LIFESAVING GIFT

—Steffie-Ann Dujon

Use this simple gift to remind people of what Jesus came to do for us.

1. Cut a piece of paper to be a tag on your gift and make a hole at the top corner big enough to fit a ribbon through.
2. Write the message "Jesus Is a Lifesaver" on the paper. Then decorate your tag. (You can also write Bible verses on the tag.)
3. Cut a square of gift wrapping paper that is big enough to fit some LifeSavers candies in the center (about 12" x 12").
4. Place some candies in the middle of the paper and gather the edges together. Slip the ribbon through the hole in the tag and tie it around the top of the "bag."

You can give this gift to family and friends or people around your neighborhood. (For those who can't eat candy, make some cards to give to them!)

STORIES IN SONG

—Gail Pelley

SABBATH ACTION BLAST 15

Each participant in this often funny activity needs a church hymnal or other Christian songbook. Each person or group must write a story using just song titles and lines from songs. To make it easier, you can have a minimum number of titles and lines that must be used in the story instead of writing the entire story from song words. When time is up, read the stories aloud and vote for the best one.

Take a trip down the Cacapon River in a kayak camping along the way.

Jonathan
age 14

Hoop Raise

—Samuel Nadarajan

For this cooperative exercise you need a hula hoop and five or more players.

Get several people around the hula hoop, which is lying flat on the floor. Each person sticks his or her index finger under the hula hoop. At the count of three, the players raise the hoop evenly above the ground, keeping it aligned with the floor. It is harder than it sounds!

After you've tried the activity, discuss what can be done to keep the hoop straighter. Whose fault is it for making the hoop unlevel?

Players may think that the person with the highest finger on the hoop is causing the hoop to be unbalanced. But the blame does not always go to the obvious. Notice what happens when that person takes their finger off the hoop. The hula hoop stays at the same angle, supported by the two next-highest fingers.

This game shows the importance of teamwork, because everybody needs to move at the same rate for the activity to succeed. Try it a few times until you master your team technique! Follow up with a worship discussion of how we as Christians can act in unison to accomplish God's work. What could happen if we begin blaming each other for the church's problems?

WORD DETECTIVES

—Sara Thompson

This game can be played with any number of players. Everyone needs a Bible, preferably all the same version.

Players decide who the first "finder" will be. That person looks in the Bible and picks a key word. All players then have to find the word anywhere in the Bible without using a concordance. The first person to find it gets to be "finder" in the next round.

For example, if the word is "king," the answer could be Isaiah 7:6; Daniel 2:2; Acts 25:13; or a lot of other texts.

Have fun sleuthing the Scriptures!

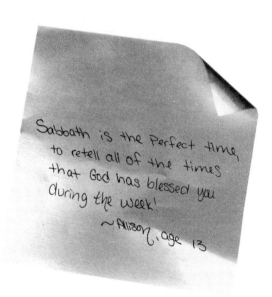

Sabbath is the perfect time to retell all of the times that God has blessed you during the week!

~Allison, age 13

ANIMAL TRACKING

—Rachel Whitaker

18

Freshly fallen snow is a great place to spot the tracks of many kinds of animals—deer, rabbits, squirrels, birds, and even your pet dog or cat! Use the Internet or a library book to find out what different animal tracks look like. Then go on a track-finding mission. Wooded areas or parks are good places to look.

Once you've found some tracks, try following them to see where they go. Look for clues as to what the animal was doing. For example, squirrel tracks leading to a hole in the snow, with bits of dirt and debris scattered around, show that the animal dug up one of its buried nuts.

You may also see scat (droppings), spots where an animal dug a burrow or hollowed out a resting place in the snow, and trails used by a group of animals.

If it doesn't snow where you live, look for tracks in mud near a pond or river, or in sand on a beach.

JESUS' SECRET AGENTS

—Victoria West

19

Have you ever wanted to spy on people or do things secretly? You can be a secret agent and serve Jesus at the same time!

To play "Jesus' Secret Agents" with your family, decorate the top of a poster board however you wish. Then make a graph on it with a couple dozen squares big enough to put a sticker in each.

Next, put every family member's name on individual slips of paper and find a bowl, cup, etc., to draw them from. Also print "Jesus' Secret Agent Was Here" on small strips of paper to give to each member of the family.

When finished, gather everyone together and have each person draw a name. Make sure no one gets their own name. You are a "secret agent" for the person whose name you drew. During the week, find nice things to do for that person. Do your good deeds secretly! Leave behind a "Jesus' Secret Agent Was Here" slip as evidence. As soon as you're finished, place a sticker in one of the squares on the chart. The sticker chart should mysteriously start to fill up, providing even further evidence that secret agents have been at work!

At the end of the week, have everyone try to guess their "secret agent." Then reveal yourselves and draw new names. You can redraw names every week.

c'mon Dad, no videos?!
...ll we do?   Is it over yet?

WHAT TI

HO HU

NE

...ousin doesn't

SHABBAT DINNER

—Rebecca Oliva

Jewish people have many special Sabbath traditions. My family uses some of them to celebrate the day. Every Friday night we have an Erev Shabbat dinner at our home. This is Hebrew for Sabbath evening. Our whole family eats together, and sometimes we have a guest.

My father starts the evening by thanking Yahweh (God's name as it appears in the original Hebrew language of Scripture) for His Shabbat. My little brother and sister sing a song. Then my mother lights two candles that represent Creation and redemption. My mother says a prayer, blessing (thanking) Yahweh for saving us through Yahushuah (Jesus' name in the Hebrew language), sanctifying (helping us become more like Him) us as we honor His commandments, and commanding us to be a light to the world. My father then prays for my mother and us kids, and my mother prays for my father.

Next my father pours grape juice into a pretty glass and blesses (praises) Yahweh for the grape juice. Then he holds one of the two loaves of challah bread (two because the Hebrews gathered two servings of manna on Friday morning to prepare for Shabbat). My little brother blesses Yahweh for bringing the bread from the earth. Next my mother says the Aaronic blessing (Numbers 6:24-26) in Hebrew, and my father says it in English.

Then we eat. My mom serves a meal that everybody likes, plus dessert. We have fun just being together and talking.

MAKE A VIDEO

—Sarah Nadarajan

Involve your friends in creating a video that will attract young people! Choose a Bible story that you would like to act out on video. Start by introducing the show. Read a Bible verse that tells the audience what your theme is about. Present a nature nugget that ties in with your lesson. Show a simple cooking item that kids can easily make at home. Include singing somewhere in the lineup. Puppets are another fun feature. Finally, at the end, present the Bible story or other skit. If you don't have time to memorize lines, have someone narrate the story.

Find someone to help you videotape the show.

Examples:

Announcer: "Welcome! I'm glad that you can tune in to [name of program]. Here you'll learn practical lessons that can help you every day. This time we'll focus on your commitment to Jesus. He's promised, 'Him that cometh to me I will in no wise cast out' [John 6:37]. Make a decision to follow Him as we pray."

Nature Nugget (show a stuffed elephant or a photo of the real thing): "Elephants stick together in large herds. Not one baby tries to wander without their mother knowing. When trouble comes, and tigers, hyenas, or jaguars try to jump on the babies, the adult elephants form a circle of protection so that the predators can't attack the young ones. Even though the baby is not theirs, they still try to protect it."

Enjoy!

82

SWEET HEARTS

—Kim Kasch

This Scandinavian Christmas tradition works great for the Valentine season, too! These woven paper hearts are still made as holiday gifts among many Danes, Swedes, and Norwegians.

To make a Sweet Heart, use gift wrap or basic construction paper to cut two rectangles, each measuring 5½" x 8" (you can make each rectangle a different color). Fold each rectangle in half and then in half again so that each one measures 2¾" x 4". Round off the edges of the open top of each rectangle with scissors to form the top of the heart. From the other end, make two straight cuts 2¾ inches long and equally spaced apart. Now slide the two rectangles into each other at right angles. You should be able to see your heart taking shape now! Weave the sides of the heart together, one side at a time, by interlocking the "legs" of each rectangle. Then tape down the ends of the legs.

To make a "basket handle" for your paper heart, cut a thin slice of paper and glue it to the inside rim of the front and back of the heart.

Fill each heart with a cookie or some other treat and give it to a special person—any day!

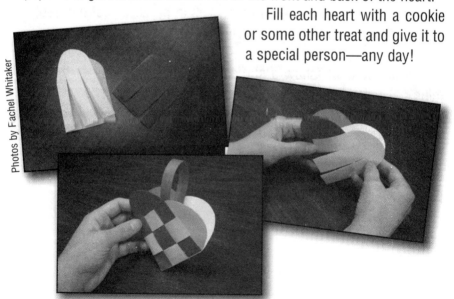

Photos by Rachel Whitaker

NAME YOUR BID

—William L. Gailliard

Here is a fun way to see how many Bible names you know. Two or four players are needed.

First, create 52 cards or paper slips, each with a letter (two complete sets of the alphabet). Label the letters F, Q, V, W, X, and Y as "miracle cards."

To play, shuffle the cards and deal all the cards out. The person to the left of the dealer picks one of their cards and has first bid. Bidding means saying how many characters you think you know from the Bible whose names start with that letter. Miracle cards may be used as any letter.

The other players then state their bids. The player with the highest bid starts naming. Maximum stall is 30 seconds; after that their turn is up, and the person with the next-highest bid must try to name different Bible people up to the number in their bid. The player who succeeds in filling their bid earns points for all the names stated up to that point.

The more players who have to try, the more points the successful player will get. The first player gets one point per name; the second player gets two points per name; and so on.

For example, player 1 picks A and bids 5, but names only Adam and Abraham. Player 2, who bid 3, names three additional people whose names start with A. Player 2 gets one point for each of player 1's names plus two points for each of their own names, for a total of eight points.

To order this game already made and in a plastic case, contact Bill Gailliard at levi35234@yahoo.com or call 1-334-328-7002.

SENSELESS STRUCTURES

—Samuel Nadarajan

Divide the participants into three equal groups. Give each group some type of building material (blocks, Legos, K'NEX, etc.). Each group must have the same material and amount. You'll also need blindfolds.

First, have each group eliminate one of the senses. For example, one group can't use the hand they write with and must hold it behind their back; another group must wear blindfolds so that they can't see; and another group can't speak.

On "Go," the groups must build some type of building that you choose. Once every group is finished, compare the results. Ask them how hard or easy it was to accomplish their task.

Now divide the people into three groups again, but this time one third of each group will be blindfolded, one third can't use the arm they write with, and one third can't speak. Again have them build a structure.

At the end, ask them if it was better than the first time. Read 1 Corinthians 12:12-20 and discuss how we as a church can work together, building on our individual abilities.

OUTER SPACE COLLAGE

—Kay Rizzo

You will need:
black or dark-blue poster board
white glue
regular or glossy computer paper
computer with Internet access and color printer

Directions:
1. Find texts in the Bible that talk about stars, night sky, planets, etc. (for example, Psalm 8:3; Isaiah 40:26; Revelation 22:16).
2. Print out the verses in an interesting font.
3. Print out pictures from the Internet that correspond with the texts chosen. Sources for outer space photos include:
   • http://hubble.nasa.gov
   • http://hubblesite.org/newscenter
   • http://www.seds.org/hst
4. Arrange pictures and text on poster board and glue in place.

Spread the Word!

—Emma Knight

Making a newsletter or mini-newspaper for your friends and family is a great idea for a rainy, snowy, or hot Sabbath afternoon.

The newspaper doesn't have to be long; it could be just a page or two. Some things to include in your Sabbath newspaper are stories; a Bible study on a topic such as Creation, prayer, or Jesus' second coming; a Bible puzzle and/or game; and a fun craft. A cartoon that portrays a Christian character trait would be fun too!

Illustrate your newspaper with photos or your own drawings. Add the artwork in your computer program, stick photos on with glue, or draw pictures on your newspaper.

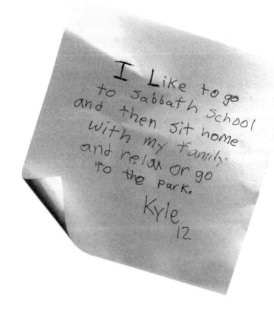

I Like to go to Sabbath School and then sit home with my family and relax or go to the park.

Kyle 12

fUN SERViCE PROJECTS

—Randy Fishell

Here are a few easy and fun service projects to do with your Sabbath school pals or another group. Add your own special touches—or come up with an even better idea!

* *Friendship door-hanger bags.* Stuff some plastic bags (the kind you can hang on doorknobs) with such items as: a seed packet, pencil, pen, notepad, a couple of Seventh-day Adventist magazines (such as *Vibrant Life* and *Message* [for adults] and *Guide* and *Insight* [for kids and teens]), individually wrapped candies or granola bars, etc. Include a handwritten note from your junior or teen group.

* *Free lemonade station.* Get permission to set up a lemonade stand in a park or near a walking, jogging, or hiking trail. Offer free water or lemonade to passersby. Have napkins and wet wipes available as well. (And a trash bag!)

* *Sidewalk serenade.* By your age you should know at least a few Christian songs by heart! Find a guitarist, and ask an adult to haul your troupe to an appropriate sidewalk or other public area and provide passersby with some great Sabbath music! Gain permissions beforehand as necessary. (Another fun option is to make this into a non-Christmas season "caroling" event. Why wait until it's freezing outside to hit the local neighborhood?)

* *Artwork giveaway.* If you like to draw, spend some time producing some artwork that honors God's creation. Make simple matting-type frames for your artwork. Have an adult take you to a nursing home or other facility and give your stunning art pieces away to the residents.

BiblE RELAY

—Shawn Robertson

This active game lets you learn about the Bible and get exercise. Form three or more teams with four people in each. Number the players on each team.

Go to a wide-open area. Form four lines of players, with one person from each team in each line. For example, player 1 from each team will stand in line 1. Put these lines in separate parts of the field. Have an extra person (not part of any team) by each line with a list of Bible questions to ask the players.

The extra person in line 1 asks all the players in that line a Bible question. The first person to answer correctly runs to line 2 and tags their teammate. (This is the team C player in the example.) Then the players in line 2 will be asked a question, and again the first person to answer correctly runs to the next line to tag a teammate. The catch is that players in lines 2-4 cannot answer until they've been tagged.

Meanwhile the people in line 1 get asked questions until the last person is gone. The same process repeats in each line. The first team to finish is the winning team.

LINE 1	LINE 2
◯	◯
Extra person	Extra person
Team A, Player 1 ◯	A2 ◯
Team B, Player 1 ◯	B2 ◯
Team C, Player 1 ◯ →	C2 ◯

Example of first two lines.

Make about 50 paper cards. On each card, write a person, place, thing, animal, idea, action, or descriptive word—anything you can think of. Shuffle the cards and distribute them equally to each player.

Choose one player to start. The starting player calls out a word from the Bible—person, place, thing, action, etc. Then the rest of the players choose one of their cards that is most related to the called-out word. They hold out their card for everyone to see. For example, if the called-out word was "Noah," players might choose words such as "boat," "water," or "dove." If none of your cards really fit, you have to make up a reason that one of them is related!

The starting player decides which card is most related to the called-out word. The person with the best word gets one point. Cards can be used only once.

Take turns calling out words. The player with the most points at the end of the game wins!

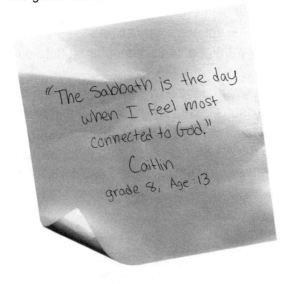

"The Sabbath is the day when I feel most connected to God."

Caitlin
grade 8, Age: 13

FAMILY TIME FUN

—Randy Fishell

Family is important to God. Here's a fun way to enjoy memories of good, not-so-hot, wacky, and other times you've spent with your family!

Write the following on slips of paper:

• Share a memory from a family vacation.
• Tell about your very first job.
• What is your favorite family recipe?
• Tell about someone who had a positive influence on you when you were young.
• Share a memory about a pet.
• Name three people you want to spend time with in heaven and tell why.
• What is something you think we should be praying more about as a family?
• What is something about your local church you wish you could change?
• Share a holiday memory.
• Tell about a time you were very scared.
• What do you want people to remember about you after you're dead?
• What is your favorite place in your house, and why?

Add other questions and items so that you end up with about 20 slips of paper. Place them in a bowl. Gather the family together and have one person draw a slip of paper from the bowl and share their response. Go clockwise until you've used up all the slips of paper or your laugh muscles get sore, whichever comes first.

STORY
OBSTACLE COURSE

—Eric Hautbois

Create an obstacle course by setting up chairs, mats, pillows, and other objects around your house in a zigzag path. Then decide what you need to do to get past each obstacle—for example, crawling under or jumping over an object. (You can play this game outdoors if the weather permits.)

On index cards, write a Bible story so that one part is on each card. (You can also make up your own Sabbath-appropriate story to write on the cards, or use a story from *Guide*.) Randomly place one index card next to each obstacle.

To play the game, race through the course, picking up a card each time you successfully pass an obstacle. At the end of the course, have all players help you unscramble the story and read it aloud!

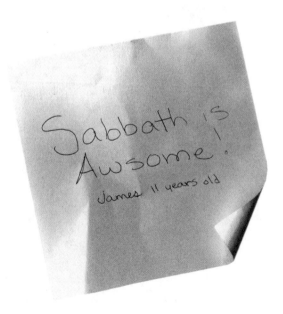

C'mon Dad, no videos?!
What'll we do?

Is it over yet?

WHAT ?

HO HU

NE

cousin doesn't

Sneaky David

—Kevin Gutierrez

Take a chair and have a blindfolded person sit on it. Put something under the chair, such as an apple or balloon. Then have some people try to sneak up as quietly as possible and take the item that is under the chair without getting caught. Make sure the blindfolded person has a small stick to try to tag the players. If the stick touches a person, that person is out!

In this game you will experience how David must have felt trying to sneak up on King Saul. Read in 1 Samuel 24 and 26 about the two times David did this.

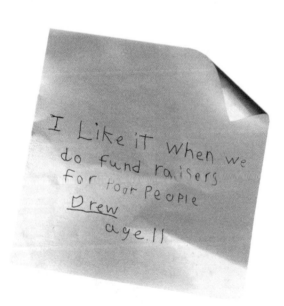

CRAZY CHARADES

—Adapted from www.partygamecentral.com

For this game you need at least six people. Ahead of time, the host writes on slips of paper several scenes to be acted out in charade fashion. Select topics from Sabbath-honoring categories such as Bible events, things done in a church, nature, etc. Examples: the princess finding Baby Moses in the basket; a deacon taking up the offering; a bird feeding its babies.

Select four players for the first round. Player 1 is given a scene to act out. The other three players are sent out of the room. When player 1 is ready to perform, player 2 is brought in to watch. After watching the scene (without being told what it is), player 2 must then act it out for player 3 by copying player 1's performance. Player 3 must then perform it for player 4.

Player 4 can make three guesses of what the scene is supposed to depict. If he/she can't figure it out, the audience can guess once. Be prepared for laughs!

Rock Art

—Dustin Radclin

On a day that is nice and sunny, go for a walk on the beach and look for flat, smooth rocks. Then when it's a rainy Sabbath day, you can use acrylic paint to paint flowers, stars, animals, or any designs you want on the rocks. (First make sure the rocks are clean and dry.) These pretty rocks make nice gifts.

Music in Action

—Rachel Whitaker

Can't sing or play an instrument? No problem—you can still use music to praise God. Try these ideas:

1. Choose a Christian song that tells a story. With friends or family, create a silent drama to go along with the words. Perform your musical drama accompanied by a recording of the song.
2. Use books or Internet resources to learn sign language for the words of a song. These actions can powerfully reinforce the meaning of the lyrics. By yourself or with a group, sign the words as your audience listens to the recorded song.
3. Make up fun motions for a kids' song you know from church. Teach the motions to a group of younger kids.

WHERE IN THE WORLD?

—Adapted from Around the World game
(www.funandgames.org)

96

This game can be played indoors or outside.

Have an adult create a list of at least 12 events from Christian history that took place in various countries around the world. Some of the events should be well known, others more challenging.

Post the names of these countries in different locations throughout your playing area.

To play, the leader calls out one of the events on the list. Players then run to the country in which they think the event occurred. Anyone who ends up in the wrong country is out of the game. The winner is the player or players who stay in the game the longest.

Optional play: The leader awards one point to all players who go to the correct country. Those who were incorrect do not receive a point but stay in the game.

Bible Password

—Katrina Pepper

97

A fun game to play on Sabbath is Bible Password. Two sets of two people sit back to back. The two players facing one direction have a card with the name of a person, place, or thing in the Bible or other Sabbath-appropriate source or category. They take turns giving one-word clues to their partner behind them. The first person to say the name on the card gets a point for their team. Then the players on the other side give clues for another name. The first team to get 15 points wins.

RiCE-ARRANGE

—Corbin Clark

SABBATH ACTION BLAST 98

You'll need:
- *uncooked rice*
- *two or three pie tins*
- *a lightweight table*
- *slips of paper*
- *watch or clock*

Setup: Divide into teams of two or three each. Set out pie tins. Pour the rice in the middle of the table. Write out some biblical items, such as boat, dove, temple, angel, etc., on the slips of paper.

The rules: Each person may touch only one piece of rice at a time.

How to play: Hand out the slips of paper and give each team a couple of minutes to plan their strategy. On "Go," the teams use the rice to illustrate their word in the pie tin. (This can get a bit messy, so keep a vacuum on hand!)

After the allotted time (three to four minutes), everyone stops their activity. Players try to guess what word or scene is being depicted.

the sun
n yet? ¿Cuándo es?
what can we do? I don't
This is ...ing.
SABBATH ACTION BLAST
99

BIBLE JEOPARDY
—Cody Edie

This game is like the TV quiz show *Jeopardy*, only with a Bible theme (or other Sabbath-honoring topic). Pick a host. The host will write Bible categories and points on a blackboard, whiteboard, or poster board. The host will also make clues for each category and point value. Put two bonus questions, worth double points, in each round.

The first player selects a category and point value, and the host reveals the corresponding question. The player who answers correctly gets the points the question was worth. But if the player misses the question, the points are deducted from their score. Of course, in true *Jeopardy*-like fashion, players must phrase their answer as a question!

At the end of the last round you can have a bonus round with one question. Each player will say how many of their points they want it to be worth. The player with the most points at the end of the game wins.

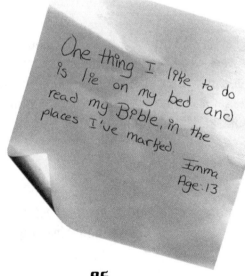

One thing I like to do is lie on my bed and read my Bible, in the places I've marked.
—Emma
Age: 13

DON'T GET LOST

—Adapted from www.users.bigpond.com

You can find your way home with a watch! (Sorry, digital watches won't work.) Here's how to do it:

- Grab a blade of grass or use a match as a pointer.
- Hold your watch horizontally (as you would a compass), with the hour hand pointing toward the sun.
- Lay the blade of grass or match across the middle of your watch, halfway between the hour hand and the 12. The grass blade or match will then be pointing south! (You'll have to figure out where to go from there!)

FACTORY BOOK

—Joe Remick

Take The Factory on the back of a *Guide* and copy down interesting facts every week. After about a month you can compile your collection into a booklet. Draw pictures or print photos from the Internet to illustrate the facts. Share your booklet with your friends. This could become your Sabbath afternoon hobby!

For more great Sabbath Action Blast activities, go to
www.guidemagazine.org